The Official Dichotomy of Leadership Companion Workbook
Published under Jocko Publishing

US Edition Manufactured in the United States of America

www.jockopublishing.com
www.echelonfront.com

Library of Congress cataloging-in-publications data
The Official Extreme Ownership Companion Workbook

Library of Congress Registration

ISBN: 979-8-9871452-0-3

Facilitated by: Jocko Publishing and Echelon Front

First Paperback Edition

9 10 8 7 6 5 4 3 2 1

1. Business
2. Self Help Techniques

OFFICIAL
COMPANION WORKBOOK

THE
DICHOTOMY
OF
LEADERSHIP

JOCKO WILLINK AND LEIF BABIN

JOCKO PUBLISHING

THE MOST SUCCESSFUL LEADERS...
BALANCE THEIR APPROACH

THERE are countless dichotomies that you will face as a leader. A dichotomy is a division or contrast between two things that are or are represented as being opposed. In other words, two opposing forces that pull against each other. Achieving the proper balance in each of the many Dichotomies of Leadership is the most difficult aspect of leadership. The twelve dichotomies covered only represent a fraction of the numerous dichotomies you will face as a leader, but understanding how to recognize and address these twelve common dichotomies will enable you to better process, analyze, and apply these leadership principles to your battlefield, in whatever arena that might be, whether leading in combat, business or life.

This workbook is not meant to replace the book "The Dichotomy of Leadership", but as a complementary resource that takes the principles from that book and provides a platform for review, interaction, and discussion, which will drive a deeper understanding of the principles for individuals and an increased alignment around the concepts inside organizations.

The workbook not only follows the same path as "The Dichotomy of Leadership", but also aligns with our online training platform, The Extreme Ownership Academy (academy. echelonfront.com), allowing leaders and teams to learn information from a variety of angles and through different media platforms.

While there is no stringent methodology on how to utilize the workbook, it was structured to be as simple and straightforward as possible: The recommended path is to start at the beginning, review the principles of leadership in each section, and then utilize the questions and discussion points to expand comprehension and connect the principles to the actual leadership scenarios you face.

Remember that effective leaders do not operate in extremes. They are constantly working to balance their approach. By utilizing this workbook to complement the book and online modules, you can begin to recognize the key indicators of out-of-balance operation and make the necessary adjustments to lead effectively. Now...

LEARN, LEAD, WIN.

TABLE OF CONTENTS

BALANCE
IN LEADERSHIP IS
CRUCIAL FOR VICTORY

INTRODUCTION
FINDING THE BALANCE

THE concept of Extreme Ownership, where leaders must take ownership of everything in their world—everything that impacts their mission—has changed the way people view leadership. Effective leaders don't cast blame on anyone or anything else. They don't make excuses. Good leaders take ownership of mistakes, determine what went wrong, develop solutions to correct those mistakes and prevent them from happening again. This mindset allows teams and leaders to enhance their effectiveness with each iteration.

The four Laws of Combat we wrote about in "Extreme Ownership" (Cover and Move, Simple, Prioritize and Execute, and Decentralized Command) have helped radically improve the performance of teams and organizations across the world in nearly every industry. But there was one big problem with "Extreme Ownership": the title. Extreme Ownership is the foundation of good leadership, but leadership seldom requires extreme ideas or attitudes. In fact, quite the opposite is true: Leadership requires balance. Every leader must walk a fine line and find the equilibrium in the dichotomy of many seemingly contradictory qualities between one extreme and another. Every behavior or characteristic of a leader can be taken too far, and when balance is lost, leadership suffers, and the team's performance rapidly declines.

Balance in leadership is crucial to victory. It must be monitored at all times and adjusted to specific situations as they arise. It is not easy to maintain the constant shift, continual modulation, and frequent adjustment necessary to balance all the dichotomies across every spectrum of leadership characteristics. Yet this skill is essential for effective leadership. The goal of "The Dichotomy of Leadership" is to help leaders overcome that struggle through examples of how to find the right balance in leadership—to moderate the idea of leading from the extremes and maintaining balance—within teams, among peers, and both up and down the chain of command. Those who master finding the equilibrium in the "Dichotomy of Leadership" will dominate their battlefield and lead their teams to victory.

INTRODUCTION: FINDING THE BALANCE
IMPLEMENTATION

1. Do you take ownership when things go wrong and implement the Laws of Combat? Give an example.

_____

_____

_____

_____

_____

2. Have you experienced a leader who took extreme actions? How did this affect you and the team?

_____

_____

_____

_____

_____

3. How do you evaluate whether decisions and actions you take are too extreme? What things do you consider about the context of the situation and how you should respond before you act?

_____

_____

_____

_____

IMMEDIATE ACTION DRILL

Write down a specific example of when you were able to overcome a difficult problem with surprising success and what you were able to accomplish. How can you replicate that success in other areas of your life?

_____

_____

_____

_____

_____

NOTES:

_____

_____

_____

_____

_____

_____

_____

_____

_____

_____

_____

_____

_____

_____

_____

IT'S NOT WHAT YOU PREACH, IT'S WHAT YOU TOLERATE, AND THAT STARTS WITH
YOU

PART I
BALANCING PEOPLE

CHAPTER 1
THE ULTIMATE DICHOTOMY

THERE are limitless dichotomies in leadership, and a leader must carefully balance between these opposing forces. None are as difficult as caring deeply for each person on the team while at the same time accepting the necessary risks to accomplish the mission and putting the long-term best interest of the overall team above any individual. A good leader builds strong relationships with their team members. While that leader would do anything for those team members, the leader must recognize there is a job to do, and that job might put those very team members at risk.

In combat, this is the ultimate dichotomy: A leader may have to send their most treasured asset—their people—into a situation that gets them wounded or killed. If their relationships are too close and they can't detach from their emotions, they might not be able to make tough choices that involve risk to their people. With that attitude, the team will get nothing done. That team fails the mission. At the other end of the spectrum, if a leader cares too much about accomplishing the mission, they may sacrifice the health and safety of their people without gaining anything. This impacts the team, who recognizes the leader as callous and no longer respects or follows them. The team will fall apart.

While not as extreme, this dichotomy reveals itself in the civilian sector as well. If leaders develop overly close relationships with their people, they may not be willing to make those people do what is necessary to complete a project or a task. They may not be willing to make hard decisions to lay off individuals with whom they have relationships, even if it is the right move for the survival of the company. And some leaders get so close to their people that they don't want to have hard conversations with them—they don't want to tell them they need improvement.

On the other hand, if a leader is too detached from the team, they may overwork, overexpose, or otherwise harm its members while achieving no significant value from that sacrifice. The leader may be too quick to fire people to save a buck, thereby developing the reputation of not caring about the team beyond its ability to support the strategic goals.

Leaders must find the balance; they must drive their team to accomplish the mission without driving them off a cliff.

CHAPTER 1: THE ULTIMATE DICHOTOMY
IMPLEMENTATION

1. Do you practice having hard conversations with your team members? Provide one recent example when you've done this.

_____

_____

_____

_____

_____

_____

_____

_____

2. When you do have hard conversations, what do they sound like? How do they go?

_____

_____

_____

_____

_____

_____

_____

_____

_____

_____

3. Where do you think you are out of balance with this dichotomy: Are you too detached or are you too close with your team members? Explain and provide a solution to how you will fix this to get back in balance.

_____

_____

_____

_____

_____

_____

_____

_____

_____

_____

4. Where would your team members say you're out of balance in this dichotomy—too detached from team members, too close, or would they say you're balanced? Explain.

_____

_____

_____

_____

_____

_____

_____

_____

_____

_____

_____

IMMEDIATE ACTION DRILL

Identify an area where you can better focus your efforts on taking care of the team so that they can better accomplish the mission. Make a plan for how you will accomplish this.

NOTES:

CHAPTER 2
OWN IT ALL, BUT EMPOWER OTHERS

THE leadership styles of micromanagement and being hands-off are obviously opposites. A micromanager tries to control every action of individuals on their team, which ultimately leads to failure because no one person can control multiple people executing a vast number of actions. Micromanagement also inhibits the growth of team members: When people become accustomed to being told what to do, they begin to await direction; initiative fades away, creativity and bold thought soon die too. The team waits for orders and only moves forward when told to do so.

The hands-off leader with a laissez-faire attitude is on the opposite end of the spectrum. This type of leader fails to provide specific direction—in some cases, almost no clear direction. Team members have grand ideas and plans. They even start to develop their own broad strategies beyond the boundaries of their responsibilities and competence. These ideas can become misaligned with the vision and goals of the company, causing this team to move in random directions.

A leader must correctly balance this dichotomy and pay attention to the team. There are some clear signs when a leader has leaned too far in one of these directions.

COMMON SYMPTOMS OF MICROMANAGEMENT:

TEAM SHOWS LACK OF INITIATIVE AND WILL NOT TAKE ACTION UNLESS TOLD TO DO SO.

TEAM DOES NOT SEEK SOLUTIONS TO ISSUES, THEY WAIT TO BE TOLD A SOLUTION.

DURING AN EMERGENCY, THE TEAM WILL NOT MOBILIZE AND TAKE ACTION.

LACK OF BOLD-AGGRESSIVE ACTION, CREATIVITY STOPS—AN OVERALL SENSE OF PASSIVITY AND FAILURE TO REACT.

CORRECTIVE ACTION FOR MICROMANAGEMENT:

PULL BACK FROM GIVING DETAILED DIRECTION; INSTEAD OF EXPLAINING HOW TO ACCOMPLISH THE MISSION, EXPLAIN THE BROAD GOALS OF THE MISSION, THE END STATE DESIRED, AND THE IMPORTANCE OF THE MISSION. ALLOW THE TEAM TO PLAN HOW TO EXECUTE THE MISSION.

CONTINUE TO CHECK THE PROGRESS OF THE TEAM, BUT REFRAIN FROM GIVING SPECIFIC GUIDANCE UNLESS THE PLAN BEING DEVELOPED WILL HAVE NEGATIVE RESULTS.

COMMON SYMPTOMS OF TOO-HANDS-OFF LEADERSHIP:

LACK OF VISION OF WHAT THE TEAM IS TRYING TO DO AND HOW TO DO IT.

LACK OF COORDINATION BETWEEN TEAM MEMBERS—EFFORTS COMPETE OR INTERFERE WITH EACH OTHER.

TEAM MEMBERS CARRY OUT UNAUTHORIZED ACTIONS, OVERSTEP THE BOUNDS OF AUTHORITY.

FAILURE TO COORDINATE OUT OF IGNORANCE: THE TEAM IS FOCUSED ON THE WRONG PRIORITY OR PURSUING SOLUTIONS THAT ARE NOT ALIGNED WITH STRATEGIC OBJECTIVES.

TOO MANY PEOPLE LEADING—INSTEAD OF PROGRESS THERE ARE LENGTHY DISCUSSIONS, INSTEAD OF ACTION THERE ARE PROLONGED DEBATE, INSTEAD OF UNITY THERE ARE FRACTURED ELEMENTS.

CORRECTIVE ACTION FOR TOO-HANDS-OFF LEADERSHIP:

SET BOUNDARIES—SIMPLE CLEAR-CONCISE GUIDANCE MUST BE GIVEN: THE MISSION, THE GOAL, THE END STATE. THE LEADER MUST DECIDE ON AND CLEARLY IMPLEMENT THE CHOSEN COURSE OF ACTION FOR THE TEAM TO FOLLOW. THE TEAM MUST BE EDUCATED ON EFFORTS BEING EXECUTED BY OTHER TEAMS.

THE LEADER MUST CLEARLY DELINEATE THE CHAIN OF COMMAND, SET ROLES AND RESPONSIBILITIES FOR THE TEAM LEADER, AND GIVE THEM PROPER AUTHORITY.

THE KEY IS BALANCE, SO TEAM MEMBERS HAVE THE GUIDANCE TO EXECUTE AND HAVE THE FREEDOM TO MAKE DECISIONS AND LEAD.

CHAPTER 2: OWN IT ALL, BUT EMPOWER OTHERS
IMPLEMENTATION

1. Do you struggle more with micromanaging or being too hands-off? Why is this difficult for you? How do you think this affects your team?

2. What can you do to get back in balance with this dichotomy? Formulate a plan for execution.

3. How would you rate your immediate boss on this dichotomy, balanced or out of balance? What can you do to help support your boss and the team better if your boss is out of balance?

IMMEDIATE ACTION DRILL

Identify two projects or tasks on which you can empower other team members to take the lead. Talk to each team member about that opportunity. Before having the conversation, role-play it with a trusted agent to ensure you are communicating effectively.

NOTES:

CHAPTER 3
RESOLUTE, BUT NOT OVERBEARING

LEADERS cannot be too lenient, but they cannot become overbearing, either. Leaders must set high standards and drive the team to achieve those standards, but they cannot be domineering or inflexible on matters of little strategic importance. To find balance, leaders must evaluate when and where to hold the line and when to allow some slack. They must determine when to listen to other team leaders and allow them ownership to make adjustments for their concerns and needs.

The term "leadership capital" helps us understand the analysis required for leaders to balance this dichotomy. Leadership capital signifies that there is a finite amount of influence that any leader possesses. It can be expended foolishly by leaders who focus on matters that are trivial and strategically unimportant. Leadership capital is acquired slowly over time through building trust and confidence with the team by demonstrating that the leader has the long-term good of the team and the mission in mind. Prioritizing those areas where standards cannot be compromised and holding the line there while allowing for some slack in other, less critical areas is a wise use of leadership capital.

The most important explanation a leader can give to the team is "Why". When a leader must hold the line and enforce standards, it must always be done with the explanation of why it is important, why it will help accomplish the mission, and what the consequences are for failing to do so. Never say, "Because I said so." Doing so will result in more pushback and difficulty getting the team to achieve the standards you are trying to enforce.

Leaders must be resolute where it matters but never overbearing, never inflexible and uncompromising on matters of small importance to the overall good of the team and the strategic mission.

CHAPTER 3: RESOLUTE, BUT NOT OVERBEARING
IMPLEMENTATION

1. Evaluate yourself. Where do you fall within this dichotomy? Are you resolute when needed, or are you overbearing and inflexible with matters of little importance? Explain.

_____

_____

_____

_____

_____

_____

_____

_____

2. What can you do to get yourself back in balance with this dichotomy? Formulate a plan for execution.

_____

_____

_____

_____

_____

_____

_____

_____

_____

_____

3. When have you wasted your leadership capital on insignificant issues that have no impact on the strategic, long-term objectives? How will you be more strategic in how you expend leadership capital?

_____

_____

_____

_____

_____

_____

_____

_____

_____

4. Please provide an example of when you held the line on a key issue or standard being ignored or broken. Why was it important to do this?

_____

_____

_____

_____

_____

_____

_____

_____

_____

_____

IMMEDIATE ACTION DRILL

Perform a leadership capital analysis on your most recent interaction. Was it a deposit or withdrawal? If it was a deposit, describe why you think it was a deposit and make a plan for how you can continue to reinforce that mindset in future interactions. If it was a withdrawal, detail what happened and make a plan for how you can avoid this in future interactions.

NOTES:

17

CHAPTER 4
WHEN TO MENTOR, WHEN TO FIRE

MOST underperformers don't need to be fired; they need to be led. But once every effort has been made to help an underperformer improve and all efforts have failed, a leader must make the tough call to let that person go. This is the duty and responsibility of every leader.

Leaders are responsible for the output of individuals on their team. The goal of any leader is to push each person to reach their maximum potential. Humans have limitations; not every person will be suited for a particular job. Some people might need a less technical position, may not be able to handle stress, or may not work well with others. Leaders must identify where to place people so their strengths are fully capitalized.

There will be people who simply cannot perform to the required level in any capacity. Once a leader has exhausted all remedial measures through training, mentoring, and counseling, the leader then must make the tough call to remove that individual from the team. The dichotomy is balancing between taking care of people by giving them enough time and opportunity to improve to a point where they can do the job properly, and protecting the overall team by removing people from positions where they negatively impact the team and the mission. A leader must be loyal to their individual team members and take care of them, but at the same time they must be loyal to the team itself and ensure every member of the team has a positive impact on the mission.

Sometimes an underperformer simply lacks the necessary skills, capacity, or aptitude to do a job. As the leader continues investing time and resources into one person, other team members and other priorities are neglected and the team can begin to falter.

This is when leaders must bring their efforts into balance. Leaders must remember that there is a team, and the performance of the team trumps the performance of any single individual. Removing a person from the team can be one of the hardest decisions a leader has to make, but it's the right decision if it's in the best interest of the team and the mission. Just remember that most underperformers don't need to be fired, they need to be led. People often ask, "When is the right time to fire someone?" The answer: When a leader has done everything possible to get an individual up to speed without seeing results, then it's time to let that person go. Don't be too quick to fire—but don't wait too long. Find balance and hold the line.

CHAPTER 4: WHEN TO MENTOR, WHEN TO FIRE
IMPLEMENTATION

1. Identify three things you can do to better mentor other team members and share helpful experience and knowledge.

2. Do you have any team members who are underperforming? What are you doing to help them out? What kind of training, feedback, and/or support are you providing them for improvement?

3. How do you change your approach when your attempt to counsel is unsuccessful? What do you do differently the next time you escalate counseling?

4. How often do you seek feedback from your boss or other team members regarding your performance? Where would your boss or team members rate you? Where would you rate yourself as a performer: Low—Medium—High performer?

_____

_____

_____

_____

_____

_____

_____

_____

_____

_____

5. Have you ever been counseled by your boss regarding your performance? Describe how you were able to make adjustments based on their feedback.

_____

_____

_____

_____

_____

_____

_____

_____

_____

_____

_____

_____

IMMEDIATE ACTION DRILL

Identify one team member to whom you can provide better support and guidance. Make a plan for how you will engage with them to provide that counseling. Role play your interaction with a trusted agent, then have that conversation with the person you identified.

NOTES:

SECTION NOTES:

PART II
BALANCING THE MISSION

CHAPTER 5
TRAIN HARD, BUT TRAIN SMART

HARD training is critical to the performance of any team. "You train how you fight, and you fight how you train," is a common mantra that drives successful U.S. military training programs. The best training programs push teams hard, far beyond their comfort zones, so the team can learn from their mistakes in training and avoid making those mistakes in real life.

Training must be hard. It must simulate realistic challenges and apply pressure on decision-makers. If training doesn't push the team beyond the limits of what is easy, then the team will never develop the capacity to take on greater challenges. Training is designed to make the team better and enable its members to function in realistic conditions they might face. The training can't be so difficult that it demoralizes participants to the point where they fail to learn. Leaders must find the balance with training and focus on realism, fundamentals, and repetition.

Training must be realistic, and scenarios should be based on scenarios that the team is likely to encounter in real life. The takeaways should be immediately applicable to the team's mission. Training should push the team into uncomfortable situations in which they aren't sure what to do. Role-play scenarios and rehearsing for likely contingencies are great training opportunities in the business world.

Training must focus on the fundamentals. While it's important to innovate and adapt, some basic tactics do not change. This is true in any business or area of life. Often people want to skip through the basic fundamentals into what they call "advanced tactics." Advanced tactics are worthless if a team can't do the basics well. A good training program develops the foundation of basic fundamentals.

Training must be repetitive. Training isn't just for new hires. A good training program must be continuous so that skills don't atrophy, and individuals and teams continue to improve with each iteration of training.

Take Extreme Ownership of training. Don't wait for someone else to build a training program. Seize the initiative on your own to train yourself and train those around you. The best training programs are driven from the bottom up by the front-line leaders who are closest to the action and lessons learned. Utilize the most accomplished members of the team to drive training programs. Good training is essential to the success of any team. Building frequently occurring training into the schedule is the most effective way to improve the team's performance. The key to great training is balance: Hard training is essential, but smart training is crucial to maximize learning and efficiency.

CHAPTER 5: TRAIN HARD, BUT TRAIN SMART
IMPLEMENTATION

1. Does your organization have a training program (not just for new hires)? If yes, what works? If no, what can you do to start designing and implementing one?

_____

_____

_____

_____

_____

_____

_____

_____

2. What can you do to make a training program better? Have you given any input on things that could be incorporated into the training program? Explain.

_____

_____

_____

_____

_____

_____

_____

_____

_____

3. What kinds of role-play scenarios or other training opportunities could be especially useful for your team? How and when can you run this training?

_____

_____

_____

_____

_____

_____

_____

_____

_____

4. What are the basic fundamentals within your job that team members should know? Identify 3-5 fundamentals and design training scenarios to teach/practice these.

_____

_____

_____

_____

_____

_____

_____

_____

_____

_____

_____

_____

_____

IMMEDIATE ACTION DRILL

Write down the next meeting you have where the majority of your team will be together (physically or virtually), and make a plan for how you will incorporate one training opportunity during that meeting. If your team does not meet regularly, work to find a time when you could all meet to synchronize and train.

NOTES:

CHAPTER 6
AGGRESSIVE, NOT RECKLESS

PROBLEMS should never be expected to solve themselves. Leaders must get aggressive, take action, and implement a proper solution. Being passive and waiting for a solution to appear often causes a problem to escalate out of control. An aggressive mindset should be the default setting of any leader. Default: Aggressive. When leaders understand the commander's intent (the overarching purpose, strategic goal and desired end state) and the parameters within which they can make decisions, they can execute. This means taking action that supports the commander's intent and the strategic vision, aggressively executing to overcome obstacles, capitalizing on immediate opportunities, accomplishing the mission, and winning. For decisions that are outside the parameters within which they can make decisions, good leaders still provide a recommended solution up the chain of command for approval.

By "aggressive," we mean "proactive." We DO NOT mean getting angry, losing your temper, or being aggressive toward other people. Leaders must always be professional when interacting with subordinates, peers, and senior leadership, and when representing the organization to external players. The aggression that wins on the battlefield, in business, and in life is directed toward solving problems, achieving goals, and accomplishing the mission.

It is critical to balance this Default: Aggressive mindset with careful analysis to make sure that risks have been calculated and mitigated. To be overly aggressive, without critical thinking, is to be reckless. That recklessness can lead the team into disaster and put the greater mission in peril. To disregard prudent counsel when someone with experience urges caution, to dismiss significant threats, or to fail to plan for likely contingencies is foolhardy. It is bad leadership.

A chief contributing factor to recklessness is "the disease of victory." This happens when a few battlefield successes result in overconfidence in a team's own tactical prowess while underestimating the capabilities of an enemy or competitor. This is a problem not just for combat leaders, but for business leaders and teams anywhere. It's the leader's duty to fight against this victory disease so that the team never gets complacent. The risk of any action as well as the risk of inaction must be carefully weighed against the potential rewards.

The dichotomy between being aggressive but utilizing caution and prudence must be balanced. So be aggressive, but never reckless.

CHAPTER 6: AGGRESSIVE, NOT RECKLESS
IMPLEMENTATION

1. When do you tend to take action without calculating the associated risks? What's your plan to fix this?

_____

_____

_____

_____

_____

_____

_____

2. Do people within your organization know and understand the strategic mission and the purpose, goal, and end state you are all trying to achieve? Do team leaders and team members take action within their scope of responsibility? Explain.

_____

_____

_____

_____

_____

_____

_____

_____

_____

3. When you don't have a lot of information, how can you move forward while still mitigating risk?

_____

_____

_____

_____

_____

_____

_____

_____

_____

_____

4. Do you ever visibly lose your temper with your people? If so, what will you do to prevent this from happening going forward? Explain.

_____

_____

_____

_____

_____

_____

_____

_____

_____

_____

_____

IMMEDIATE ACTION DRILL

Identify one initiative you have been hesitant to take on. Make a plan for how you can aggressively work to implement a solution, and document the risks associated with your idea. Take action on this initiative using the smallest iterative step you can pull out of your plan.

NOTES:

CHAPTER 7
DISCIPLINED, NOT RIGID

WHILE "Discipline Equals Freedom" is a powerful tool for both personal and team development, excessive discipline can stifle free thinking among team members. The more discipline a team exercises, the more freedom that team will have to maneuver by implementing small adjustments to existing plans. When facing a mission or a task, instead of having to craft a plan from scratch, a team can follow Standard Operating Procedures (SOPs) for the bulk of the plan. Defined SOPs are a line to deviate from and they allow the freedom to act quickly based on those procedures.

But there must be a balance. In some organizations, there are leaders who put too many SOPs in place. They create strict processes that inhibit their subordinate leaders' ability to think. This can adversely impact the team's performance and the mission.

Disciplined procedures must be balanced with the ability to apply common sense to an issue, with the power to break from SOPs when necessary, with the freedom to think about alternative solutions, apply new ideas, and make adjustments to processes based on the reality of what is actually happening. If discipline is too strict, team members cannot adjust, cannot adapt, and cannot use their most precious asset—their brains—to quickly develop customized solutions to unique problems for which the standard solution might not work.

And when taken to an extreme, too much discipline—too many processes and too many standard procedures—completely inhibits and stifles the initiative of subordinates. Instead of stepping up and making necessary changes, leaders confined to strict procedures will simply follow the procedures even when those procedures are obviously leading to failure.

So, as a leader, it is critical to balance the strict discipline of standard procedures with the freedom to adapt, adjust, and maneuver to do what is best to support the overarching commander's intent and achieve victory. For leaders in combat, business, and life, be disciplined, but not rigid.

CHAPTER 7: DISCIPLINED, NOT RIGID
IMPLEMENTATION

1. Do you have rigid standard operating procedures (SOPs) inside your organization? What are they? How can you make these processes more efficient and effective for the organization?

2. Do your leaders and front-line workers have the ability to make adjustments within SOPs while working on a project? Explain.

3. How often are SOPs reviewed and updated within your organization? Where does the input come from to adjust your organization's SOPs?

_____

_____

_____

_____

_____

_____

_____

_____

_____

_____

4. How often do you conduct training on SOPs? Do front-line leaders and employees understand why these SOPs are in place?

_____

_____

_____

_____

_____

_____

_____

_____

_____

_____

_____

_____

IMMEDIATE ACTION DRILL

Identify one SOP that needs to be updated. Work with others who also utilize the SOP to determine changes and why they are necessary. Then, present the proposed update up the chain for approval.

NOTES:

CHAPTER 8
HOLD PEOPLE ACCOUNTABLE, BUT DON'T HOLD THEIR HANDS

ACCOUNTABILITY is an important tool for leaders to utilize; however, it should not be the primary tool. It must be balanced with other leadership tools, such as making sure people understand the why, empowering subordinates, and trusting they will do the right thing without direct oversight.

Leaders often get the idea that accountability can solve everything—and in a sense, they're right. If a leader wants to ensure a subordinate follows through with a task, the leader can inspect repeatedly to confirm that the task gets done. With enough oversight, task completion can achieve 100 percent success. Therefore, leaders often want to use accountability to fix problems: It is the most obvious and simple method. A task is given to a subordinate; the leader watches the subordinate do the task; the leader inspects the task once it's complete. There is almost no room for error.

Unfortunately, there is also almost no room for the leader to do anything else besides monitor the progress of that specific subordinate. If there are multiple subordinates with multiple tasks, a leader very quickly becomes physically incapable of inspecting them all. While focused down the chain of command, the leader will have no ability to look up and out—up toward senior leadership to build relationships and influence strategic decisions, and out toward the strategic mission to anticipate future operations.

Instead of using accountability as the primary tool of leadership, leaders should implement it as one of many leadership tools. Leaders must ensure the team understands the why, and that members have ownership of their tasks and the ability to make adjustments as needed. Team members need to understand the importance of their specific task and the consequences of failure.

Accountability should be used to hold the line and uphold the standards where it matters most. This is another dichotomy nested in accountability: there are absolutely cases when accountability should be used. If a subordinate is not performing to standard, despite understanding the why, knowing the impact on the mission, and being given ownership, then the leader must hold the line. That method is accountability. The leader must drill down and micromanage tasks to get the team member on track, but the leader cannot stay there. The leader must give subordinates leeway to perform based on their own intrinsic drive because they have a better understanding of why. Use accountability as a tool when needed, but not as the sole means of enforcement. Reliance on heavy accountability consumes the leader's time and focus and stifles team members' trust, growth, and development. Balance accountability with educating the team and empowering its members to maintain standards even without direct oversight from the top. This is the hallmark of high-performing teams that dominate.

CHAPTER 8: HOLD PEOPLE ACCOUNTABLE, BUT DON'T HOLD THEIR HANDS
IMPLEMENTATION

1. How can you better balance holding others accountable and giving them space?

2. If you have subordinates, how can you ensure that your team understands the importance of their tasks and how they fit into the larger mission? If you are a front-line employee, how can you get clarity when you don't understand the why behind your tasks?

3. Does leadership in your organization allow front-line workers to make adjustments as needed? How can you lead up or down to make sure this happens effectively?

4. Where can you do a better job looking up and out at strategic objectives versus down and in on tactical details?

IMMEDIATE ACTION DRILL

Identify one person you have been micromanaging (hand-holding) recently. Make a plan for how you can begin to show more trust in their ability to get the job done. Execute that plan and adjust as needed until that person has full autonomy.

NOTES:

SECTION NOTES:

PART III
BALANCING YOURSELF

CHAPTER 9
A LEADER AND A FOLLOWER

EVERY leader must be willing and able to lead, but just as important is a leader's ability to follow. Leaders must be willing to lean on the expertise and ideas of others, and to listen and follow others, regardless of their rank or experience. If another team member has a great idea, a good leader recognizes that it does not matter who gets the credit, only that the mission is accomplished in the most effective manner possible. Confident leaders encourage junior team members to step up and lead when they put forth ideas that will contribute to mission success.

A good leader must also be a good follower of their own leader—one of the most important jobs of any leader is to support their own boss. When the debate over a particular course of action ends and the boss makes a decision, even if you disagree with the decision, you must execute the plan as if it were your own. Only if the orders coming down from senior leadership are illegal, immoral, unethical, or significantly risky to lives, limbs, or the strategic success of the organization should a subordinate leader hold fast against directives from superiors.

A good leader must also be willing to follow when others come up with a good plan to help the team win. Even if it is a more junior or less experienced member of the team, a good leader is willing to follow when others are in the best position to lead the team to victory.

A good leader must follow and support the chain of command. It may be challenging to follow a leader who is less competent, less aggressive, uncharismatic, or uninspiring. Regardless, when lawful orders from the boss or higher chain of command conflict with a leader's ideas, a subordinate leader must still be willing to follow and support the chain of command, including that of the defiant leader. Failing to follow creates an antagonistic relationship up the chain of command, which negatively impacts the willingness of the boss to take input and suggestions from the subordinate leader and hurts the team. Leaders who fail to be good followers fail themselves and their teams. When a leader is willing to follow, the team functions effectively and the probability of mission success radically increases.

CHAPTER 9: A LEADER AND A FOLLOWER
IMPLEMENTATION

1. Where inside your team or organization can you do a better job of being a leader and a follower? How can you make this happen?

_____

_____

_____

_____

_____

_____

2. How can you implement a balanced approach to leading and allowing others to lead?

_____

_____

_____

_____

_____

_____

3. Do you consider input from less senior team members? Please write down two examples where you've taken junior team members' input for consideration.

_____

_____

_____

_____

_____

_____

4. How do you support your leaders when they make a decision with which you disagree?

5. Does your leadership trust you? Does your team trust you? Explain.

6. Does your leadership value and seek your opinion for guidance? Explain.

IMMEDIATE ACTION DRILL

Identify a project or initiative you do not entirely support that you've been pushing back on or pushing your ideas in instead of supporting others. How can you be a better follower? Document a plan below and act on it.

NOTES:

CHAPTER 10
PLAN, BUT DON'T OVERPLAN

CAREFUL planning is essential to the success of any mission. In "Extreme Ownership", Chapter 9, "Plan," we wrote that mission planning meant "never taking anything for granted, preparing for likely contingencies, and maximizing the chance of mission success while minimizing the risk to the troops executing the operation." There are significant risks in both combat and business alike. In the business world, livelihoods are at stake: jobs, careers, capital, strategic initiatives, and long-term success. Leaders must manage these risks through careful contingency planning, though not every risk can be controlled.

Leaders must find balance when planning. You cannot plan for every contingency. If you try to plan for every possible contingency, you will overwhelm your team and the planning process and overcomplicate decisions for leaders. Therefore, it is imperative that leaders focus primarily on the likely contingencies that could occur during each phase of a mission or project. Select at most three or four of the most probable contingencies for each phase, along with the worst-case scenario. This will prepare the team to execute and increase the chances of mission success.

Leaders should not stray too far in the other direction either by not planning enough for contingencies. When leaders dismiss likely threats or problems that could arise, it sets the team up for greater difficulties and may lead to mission failure. Leaders must fight against complacency and overconfidence. Never forget just how much is at stake.

Each risk requires careful evaluation, weighing and balancing the risk versus the reward—the benefit to the team and to the strategic mission of a successful outcome. Careful and focused contingency plans are key to managing risks and achieving victory. It is critical for every leader to understand that to be successful, they must plan but not overplan.

CHAPTER 10: PLAN, BUT DON'T OVERPLAN
IMPLEMENTATION

1. Is your tendency to underplan or overplan? How can you move toward balancing this dichotomy?

_____

_____

_____

_____

_____

_____

_____

_____

2. Do you develop contingency plans for likely scenarios before starting a project or task? Do you try and plan for every possible scenario causing your plans to be too complex and inflexible? Explain.

_____

_____

_____

_____

_____

_____

_____

_____

_____

_____

3. Are you and your team prepared for worst-case scenarios? Explain how you will execute a contingency plan if one should occur.

_____

_____

_____

_____

_____

_____

_____

_____

_____

_____

4. Before deciding to execute, how do you weigh the risk versus reward of a situation?

_____

_____

_____

_____

_____

_____

_____

_____

_____

_____

_____

_____

IMMEDIATE ACTION DRILL

Identify an upcoming project or one currently in progress that needs more planning. Work with team members to create checkpoints to ensure progress, and contingency plans for potential problems to protect the team from failing.

_____

_____

_____

_____

_____

_____

_____

NOTES:

_____

_____

_____

_____

_____

_____

_____

_____

_____

_____

_____

_____

CHAPTER 11
HUMBLE, NOT PASSIVE

HUMILITY is the most important quality in a leader. When we had to fire SEAL leaders from leadership positions in a platoon or task unit, it was not because they weren't physically fit, or were tactically unsound. It was most often because they lacked humility. They couldn't check their ego. They refused to accept constructive criticism and did not take ownership of their mistakes. In Extreme Ownership, we dedicated an entire chapter to "Check the Ego" because humility is essential to building strong relationships up, down, and across the chain of command.

Some leaders take this too far and become humble to a fault. They become passive. When it truly matters, leaders must be willing to push back, voice their concerns, stand up for the good of their team and the mission, and provide feedback up the chain against a decision or strategy they know will endanger the team or harm the strategic mission.

This can be a difficult dichotomy to balance, but as with all the dichotomies, just the awareness that these two opposing forces exist provides a powerful tool for leaders. Leaders must be humble enough to listen to new ideas and strategic insights, and be open to implementing new tactics and strategies. A leader must also be ready to raise concerns and ask questions up the chain when there are clearly unintended consequences that would negatively impact the mission and risk harm to the team or the organization.

CHAPTER 11: HUMBLE, NOT PASSIVE
IMPLEMENTATION

1. Where do you fall on the scale of humility (from arrogant to passive)? How can you make sure you are balanced?

_____

_____

_____

_____

2. How do you usually react when given constructive criticism from your boss or teammates? Do you truly listen and make adjustments based on the feedback? List some examples of when you've done this.

_____

_____

_____

_____

_____

3. Have you ever spoken up about a decision that may have had a negative impact on the mission or team? If so, what was the result? If not, what would be some things that would cross this line for you? How could you effectively communicate why you disagree?

_____

_____

_____

_____

_____

_____

_____

IMMEDIATE ACTION DRILL

Go to a trusted team member and ask for some constructive feedback. No matter what it is, address it immediately. Document what changes you are going to implement to address that feedback here.

NOTES:

CHAPTER 12
FOCUSED, BUT DETACHED

LEADERS must be attentive to details. However, leaders cannot be so immersed in the details that they lose track of the larger strategic picture and are unable to support or provide direction to the entire team.

Leaders must be able to stand back and observe everything going on inside their team and organization, which will allow them to provide good direction all around. This also allows the leader to keep the larger, overarching goals of the mission in perspective.

When confronted with the enormity of operational plans and the intricate details within those plans, it becomes easy to get lost in the minutiae. It is crucial for leaders to pull themselves off the firing line, step back, detach, and maintain the strategic picture. Detachment is an issue with which many leaders struggle. They allow themselves to get so obsessed with the details that they lose focus on the bigger picture. It is essential for leaders to understand the importance of maintaining a detached mindset, so they can always be aware of the bigger picture.

It is imperative for leaders to understand the balance between understanding the details and becoming completely submerged and overwhelmed by them. Leaders can't get so far away—so detached—that they lose track of what's happening on the front lines. Leaders must be attentive to the details and understand the challenges the team is confronting, but they can't be obsessed with the details. Leaders should position themselves where they can best support their teams.

This is the dichotomy that must be balanced: To be engrossed in and overwhelmed by the details risks mission failure, but to be so far detached from the details that the leader can't support the team and loses control is to fail the team and fail the mission.

CHAPTER 12: FOCUSED, BUT DETACHED
IMPLEMENTATION

1. Do you effectively balance understanding the details without becoming submerged and overwhelmed by them? How can you better balance this dichotomy?

_____

_____

_____

_____

_____

_____

_____

_____

2. Can you stand back and observe everything happening within your team and organization? How can you improve your ability to detach?

_____

_____

_____

_____

_____

_____

_____

_____

_____

_____

3. Do you ever lose track of the bigger strategic plan? What can you do to prevent this?

_____

_____

_____

_____

_____

_____

_____

_____

_____

_____

4. What are some examples of how you've effectively supported your team in your position as a leader? Identify ways you can improve.

_____

_____

_____

_____

_____

_____

_____

_____

_____

_____

_____

_____

_____

_____

IMMEDIATE ACTION DRILL

During your next team meeting, focus on what is happening with your team by talking less and keeping a detached perspective. Use the information to formulate a plan to better support your team.

NOTES:

APPENDIX//
GLOSSARY OF TERMS

GLOSSARY OF TERMS

AFTER ACTION REVIEW (AAR)
Structured debrief of what happened, why it happened, and what could be done better as well as any other takeaways.

COMMANDER'S INTENT
The strategic goal of the mission or task. It is the explanation of not what to do but why, which enables leaders at every level of the team to step up and lead with Decentralized Command.

COVER AND MOVE
Teamwork. The team must work together, mutually supporting one another in order to accomplish the goal. If the team succeeds, everyone succeeds. If the team fails, everyone fails. Accomplishing the mission is the highest priority.

DECENTRALIZED COMMAND
Everyone leads. To enable this, leaders at all levels must understand the mission and the why behind the mission. They must also understand the endstate, the goal, and the parameters within which they can operate.

DICHOTOMY OF LEADERSHIP
Leaders must strive to find the right balance to be effective when two opposing forces are pulling them in different directions, and both directions are correct. Everyone is different, and everything is dynamic. Work to achieve balance every day.

DISCIPLINE EQUALS FREEDOM
There is no hack. There are no secrets, no shortcuts, no tricks. The pathway to freedom is through discipline.

EXECUTION CHECKLIST (Ex Check)
List of key tasks to complete and timelines or dates for their completion.

EXTREME OWNERSHIP
The mindset and attitude which is foundational to the best leaders and organizations; they don't make excuses, blame others or circumstances. Instead, they take ownership of mistakes and failures and implement effective solutions that get problems solved.

LEADER
To be a leader means to get a group of people to effectively execute a complex mission to accomplish strategic goals in a dynamic environment. It is directly applicable from combat leadership to leadership in the business world and life. The principles are immediately transferable to what you do, every day, in every aspect of your world.

LEADERSHIP
The most important thing on the battlefield and to the success of any organization in any situation. It is the critical difference between success and failure, winning and losing.

PRIORITIZE AND EXECUTE
You can't do everything at once. If you try, you will fail. Even if everything appears to be high priority, you still need to detach, figure out the highest priority task, and then execute to accomplish it. When things feel overwhelming, detach from emotion. Relax. Look Around. Make a Call.

READBACK
A tool to ensure communication is simple and understood by the team. Ask a team member to explain your communication back to you in their words. If they explain it correctly, you communicated effectively. If not, you have failed to communicate effectively and must explain again. Remember to take ownership of both the readback and the outcome.

ROLE-PLAY
A role play is a way to practice a conversation before you have it. Before you go to speak with someone about an issue or opportunity, you take the time to talk through exactly what you want to say with a trusted agent. That trusted agent could be a co-worker, mentor, spouse, or any person you feel you can trust to give you solid feedback and keep the conversation confidential. This allows you to be better prepared for the real conversation and ensure that what you are saying is coming across the way you intend.

SIMPLE
Plans, orders and communication must be simple, clear, and concise so that everyone understands. If your team does not understand, they can't execute.

SUBORDINATE
A junior member of the team in the rank structure of the organization. It is standard military term and does not denote any inferiority, but merely refers to organizational hierarchy.

STANDARD OPERATING PROCEDURES
(SOPs) Set of detailed instructions for completing a certain recurring task; best practice. Should be developed by the person/people completing the task and reviewed regularly for improvements.

STUDY.

EXCERPT FROM LEADERSHIP STRATEGY AND TACTICS: FIELD MANUAL BY JOCKO WILLINK

LEADERS are never good enough. A leader must be constantly improving and learning since, in any leadership job, new and unexpected challenges arise all the time and, as one continues to lead, the number of people being led increases, projects multiply in number and scope, and the overall strategic impact of the missions being led also expands.

Leadership in any chosen profession is just that—a profession. Being a leader is your life. Do everything humanly possible to know and understand everything there is about your profession and being a leader in that profession. Strive every day to learn and become a better leader…

Think about the fundamental principles of leadership and overlay them onto everything you see to expand your thinking. Cover and Move. Simple. Prioritize and Execute. Decentralized Command. Extreme Ownership. The Dichotomy of Leadership. If you look for these principles, you will see them; if you see them, you will understand them better. The better you understand them, the better you can implement them; the better you can implement them, the more you can look for them, and this cycle continues forever.

NONE OF THIS HAPPENS WITHOUT HUMILITY.

If a leader thinks they have achieved the pinnacle of leadership expertise, they are already going in the wrong direction, stagnant in their skill set, and, worst of all, unconsciously giving off the stink of arrogance. Don't let this happen. **Stay humble, and always learn.**

ECHELONFRONT.COM

EVERY CHALLENGE A COMPANY OR ORGANIZATION MAY FACE:

LEADERSHIP IS THE SOLUTION.

OUR MISSION

Echelon Front's mission is to educate, train, mentor, and inspire LEADERS and organizations to overcome challenges, seize opportunities, and achieve total victory. Utilizing lessons learned and proven in combat, we help LEADERS develop the core ACTIONS and MINDSETS necessary to tackle issues including strategy, execution, safety and risk mitigation, mission planning, innovation, team building, crisis management strategies, and cultural transformation.

OUR SERVICES

Echelon Front offers practical, experience-based solutions to complex problems based on leadership lessons learned in the military and the private sector. Using our vast experience with dynamic leadership challenges, we connect those lessons to both business and life so our clients can apply them immediately. We don't teach theory learned in a classroom. We offer a wide range of unique, customized, and personalized services designed to get your team executing at the highest level possible.

LEADERSHIP CONSULTING

    LEADERSHIP DEVELOPMENT AND ALIGNMENT PROGRAMS (LDAP)
    ASSESSMENTS AND STRATEGIC ADVISING

IN-PERSON TRAINING

    ON-SITE TRAINING—HALF-DAY, FULL-DAY AND MULTI-DAY WORKSHOPS
    KEYNOTE PRESENTATIONS

VIRTUAL TRAINING

    VIRTUAL TRAINING AND CERTIFICATION PROGRAMS—EXTREME OWNERSHIP ACADEMY
    WEBINARS AND VIRTUAL WORKSHOPS
    VIRTUAL KEYNOTE PRESENTATIONS

EXPERIENTIAL TRAINING

    EXTREME OWNERSHIP FIELD TRAINING EXERCISES (FTX)
    EXTREME OWNERSHIP MUSTER CONFERENCE
    THE ASSEMBLY: WOMEN IN LEADERSHIP—BUSINESS AND LIFE

EXTREME OWNERSHIP ACADEMY

THE EXTREME OWNERSHIP ACADEMY IS OUR VIRTUAL LEADERSHIP TRAINING PLATFORM WHERE WE APPLY AND INSTILL THE PRINCIPLES OF EXTREME OWNERSHIP AND THE LAWS OF COMBAT THROUGH SUSTAINED ONLINE LEARNING AND DIRECT LIVE INTERACTION.

ON-DEMAND LEADERSHIP TRAINING FOR YOU AND YOUR TEAM

START BY CREATING A FREE ACCOUNT AND GET INSTANT ACCESS TO THESE COURSES:

THE LEADERSHIP ASSESSMENT TEST WILL SHOW YOU WHERE YOU ARE ON YOUR LEADERSHIP JOURNEY AND, MORE IMPORTANTLY, WHERE YOUR LEADERSHIP SKILLS NEED IMPROVEMENT.

THE BARRIERS TO EXTREME OWNERSHIP COURSE, WITH JAMIE COCHRAN AND JOCKO, EXPLORES THE BARRIERS THAT HOLD US BACK FROM TAKING OWNERSHIP, AND HOW WE CAN OVERCOME THEM.

THE EXTREME OWNERSHIP FRAMEWORK COURSE, WITH DAVE BERKE AND JOCKO, TEACHES THE 5 STEPS TO TAKING EFFECTIVE OWNERSHIP IN DIFFICULT SITUATIONS AND WHEN HAVING HARD CONVERSATIONS.

CREATE A FREE ACCOUNT AT ACADEMY.ECHELONFRONT.COM

ONCE YOU COMPLETE THE FREE TRAINING EXPLORE OUR FOUNDATIONS AND STRATEGY AND TACTICS COURSES THAT ARE AVAILABLE FOR PURCHASE AT THE ACADEMY. YOU CAN ALSO JOIN OUR LIVE SESSIONS TO SOLVE YOUR INDIVIDUAL LEADERSHIP CHALLENGES.

ACCESS 30+ HOURS OF ONLINE COURSE MATERIAL THAT EACH INCLUDE:

- A COMBAT EXAMPLE FROM THE BATTLEFIELD
- OUTLINE OF THE LEADERSHIP PRINCIPLE
- APPLICATION TO BUSINESS OR INDUSTRY
- APPLICATION EXERCISES
- FINAL LEARNING CHECK

EXTREME OWNERSHIP ACADEMY LIVE SESSIONS

INTERACT DIRECTLY WITH JOCKO, LEIF, AND THE REST OF THE ECHELON FRONT LEADERSHIP INSTRUCTORS ONCE A WEEK TO DISCUSS AND SOLVE YOUR SPECIFIC LEADERSHIP CHALLENGES.

SAVE 20% WITH CODE: AMAZON20

OR SIMPLY SCAN THE QR CODE TO GET STARTED AT ACADEMY.ECHELONFRONT.COM

RECOMMENDED READING FOR THOSE THAT ARE LOOKING TO GET AFTER IT

READ.
LEAD.
WIN.

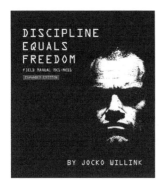

STRONGER KIDS FOR A STRONGER TOMORROW

ECHELONFRONT.COM

Made in the USA
Middletown, DE
08 September 2024

60642188R00042